The Hypochondriac's Book of Verse

by

Dulcie Levene

Illustrations by Jean deLemos

The Hypocondriac's Book of Verse

Library of Congress
Cataloging in Publication Data

ISBN 1-58235-445-6

Manufactured in The United States of America by
Watermark Press
6 Gwynns Mill Court
Owings Mills, MD 21117
410-654-0400

This book is dedicated
to
my children
and to
Nadine McCowan
and to Wendy
without whose encouragement
it would never have been written

Dulcie Levene

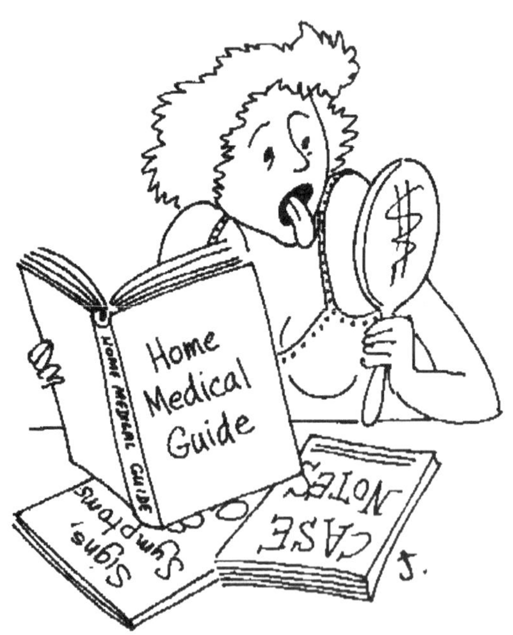

A Little Knowledge

Don't ever start to look
Inside a medical book
For there might be illnesses you shouldn't see
Looking for an explanation
Could fire imagination
And you'll find you've everything bar Housemaid's Knee!

Dulcie Levene

Nerves

A patient gets what she deserves
If she says 'Doctor, it's my nerves'
For after quite a third degree
She'll find she gets no sympathy…

Should she return (and one should be wiser)
She'll end up with a tranquilizer
And Heaven help should she persist
She's sent to a psychiatrist!

Medical Encyclopedia
Medical E
Home Doctor
Home Doctor
Symptoms of:
Cronic bronchitis,
Painful arthritus
Deep vein thrombosis
Osteoporosis
Liver infection
Kidney failure
J.

Such a Fool

I feel such a fool
For I've broken my rule
And opened a medical book
And now I am furious
That I was so curious
How I wish I'd not taken a look!

I knew from the start
What that book could impart
The fears and the terror it would bring
Now the problems I've read
Point out I should be dead
For it seems that I've got everything…

From cover to cover
I tried to discover
The horrible symptoms I've shown
And now I feel faint
For I've every complaint
That's ever been written or known.

There's chronic bronchitis
And painful arthritis
Lumbar punctures and awful injections
Then there's deep vein thrombosis
And osteoporosis
And liver and kidney infections.

From A unto Z
Every page that I read
(Some too ghastly for me to describe)
Have made it quite plain
That I could go insane
And feel fortunate I'm still alive…

I need counselling now
And I'll get it somehow
For I'm seeing my doctor today
And I'm making a list
Of some symptoms I've missed
Heaven knows what he's going to say!

BEWARE
OF
UNKNOWN
VIRUS!
J.

Virus

Have you ever felt rejected
When you've become infected
With a germ or virus hitherto unknown?
When you need a helping hand
Your friends decide that they'll disband
And you're left to fight your illness on your own…

They don't mean to disregard
They telephone or send a card
It's the isolation that you can't abide
And when your best friend Dora
Sends you flowers from 'Interflora'
Your quite grateful they arrived before you died.

Florence Nightingale it seemed
Was the one who never dreamed
Of deserting patients even with the plague
So you'll remember with a frown
The day your best friends let you down
Even though your diagnosis was quite vague.

So when you're feeling better
Write each one of them a letter
Inviting everyone to come for tea
On a placard in your hall
Inform them one and all
Not to be afraid – you're now infection free!

You'll see tears in their eyes
As they all apologise
So smile at them and say you understand
And tell them that you will
If ever they are ill
Be the first one at their door to lend a hand!

Dulcie Levene

Sharing

I have whiplash I'm sure
And I've tried to endure
This terrible pain in my neck
For I've been in a crash
And I got such a bash
That now, like the car, I'm a wreck!

My Husband's gone out
God!... did he scream and shout
And it's really quite easy to see
That if he had to choose
I would surely lose
He thinks more of that car than of me!

He's made me quite ill
So I'm making my will
And this might be the last thing I write
His love for his car
Has outstripped me by far
Is the end of our marriage in sight?

Twenty years of my life
As a wonderful wife
On the line... as I'm being compared
To a beastly machine
He keeps spotlessly clean
And he's rushed out to get it repaired...

Doctor said I'll be cured
And the car is insured
So it seems that the outlook is bright
And I've already decided
If his love is divided
I'll share him and say it's alright!

DOCTORS SURGERY
URGENT
V. URGENT

Heart

I asked myself this question
Is it heart or indigestion?
And decided I should ring the surgery
I heard the nurse exclaim
'Oh God! it's her again'
So I knew they weren't too pleased to hear from me...

My doctor looked quite grim
As I confronted him
And said 'You fear the worst at every symptom shown
I have patients every day
Who worry in this kind of way
So rest assured that you're not on your own'

As I burst into tears
He soon dispelled my fears
And said 'I've checked you well and you are quite alright
Your fears might abate
If you lose a little weight
And you know my dear... Your bra is much too tight!'

Dulcie Levene

Gallbladder

I never felt sadder
Than when my gallbladder
Decided to make itself known
To the doctor I fled
Who thoughtfully said
'I think you could have a gallstone'

How my fears grew
An operation was due
And I thought of the stitches and scars
My love life it seemed
Would be one to be dreamed
I'd look like a mutation from Mars

And then came the day
That I had my X-ray
And I shivered and shook as I waited
The nurse took my hand
For I couldn't stand
And she feared that I should be sedated.

Then three weeks went by
When I just 'Piped my Eye'
And they rang me with this information
Doctor says it's good news
So snap out of those blues
You've just had severe inflammation!

Dulcie Levene

Holidays

We're having these injections
To ward off all infections
For we're off on an exotic holiday
For Polio and Hepatitis
And in case mosquitoes bite us
We take malaria tablets every day.

I'm so full of nervous tension
Added to my apprehension
When we booked our holiday I made it clear
Exotic places out of reach
Are never nicer than our beach
I would have settled for two weeks near Bournmouth's pier…

They'll all think me an outsider
When I scream at some big spider
Who's been waiting for the day that I arrive
And I know I'll get the shakes
At cockroaches and horrid snakes
I'll be lucky if I get back home alive!

I don't want to seem ungrateful
But creepy crawlies are so hateful
And I can't imagine what we're going to eat
If it's curry or chow mein
I know that I'll abstain
So just in case I'll pack some shredded wheat!

Just because we're all insured
Doesn't mean we can be cured
It's quite likely that I'll catch something and die
So we're on the plane tomorrow
And I'm saying this with sorrow
If I don't get back you'll know the reason why!

Migraine

I'm staying in bed
I've this pain in my head
It could be severe migraine
I've tried 'Aspro'
But the pain will not go
And I think it's affecting my brain.

I've made this decision
If I get double vision
I'm going to call doctor today
For I hope it's a rumour
But I've heard a brain tumour
Can start in this terrible way.

I'm feeling so sick
If it doesn't go quick
I might have to dial 999
And I should be injected
If my eyesight's affected
Or I might have a hasty decline.

Eye drops and a lotion
Might set things in motion
Perhaps I should have an eye test
Or stay in a dark room
With my feelings of doom
And try hard to get a night's rest.

False alarm bells are ringing
So I ought to be singing
And I'm making it perfectly plain
I'm a little unsteady
But it's morning already
And I'm quite clear-headed again!

Dulcie Levene

The Menopause

I'm not feeling very jolly
In fact I'm melancholy
And I think I've put my finger on the cause
I'm filled with this depression
And I must make this confession
I think I could be in the menopause.

I'm suffering from hot flushes
Scarlet neck and bright red blushes
And I'm positive my heart has missed a beat
I absolutely dread
When it's time to go to bed
For I throw off all the clothes because of heat.

My friends say I am strange
Well... one would be in the 'change'
And I must say they're not showing much concern
They should feel honour bound
To come and rally round
And hold my hand in case I have a 'turn.'

I'm feeling agitated
And my husband's quite frustrated
I've read him books to make things more enlightening
I can't help wondering when
We're going to have a 'pause from men'
Then the menopause would not seem quite so frightening...

Cosmetic surgery
Or should I go on H.R.T.
For I've heard it's praises very highly sung
If surveys tell the truth
It recaptures long lost youth
And keeps you looking very, very young...

From the cradle to the grave
All women must be brave
So I'll do my best and with a bit of luck
I'll try hard to be brave
But I'll start to scrimp and save
And if all else fails... I'll have a 'nip and tuck.'

RIP
J.

My Doctor

It's a mystery to me
That when I talk to my G.P.
He resolutely stays unsympathetic
He doesn't concentrate at all
His gaze is fixed upon the wall
And it's obvious he thinks that I'm pathetic…

He never says 'Have a nice day'
As he sends me on my way
And there's never been a 'Hi! there' or 'Hello!'
Though I'm panicking in fear
He just doesn't seem to hear
And his milk of human kindness doesn't show…

And yet, I think that I'd expire
If he decided to retire
I feel I couldn't cope with someone new
At heart I think he's wise
Though he does fuss and criticise
And there's no one else to tell my troubles to!

So I'll bravely soldier on
Until one of us has gone
At least he knows my medical history
And although I think he's hard
I'll always send his Christmas card
And hope one day he'll send a card to me!

A-A-CHOO!
Emergency
DOCTOR
J.

A Hypochondriac......I'm Not!

I'm not a hypochondriac
Though I'm labeled one I know
I wear my badge of courage
Even though it doesn't show

The apprehension that I feel
Applies to everyone
To Kings and Queens and Presidents
It could even happen to a nun...

For one's most intimate possession
Is their body I am sure
Which they surrender to a doctor
In the hope he'll find a cure

For any ailment that assaults them
And pray he understands
That they could be sacrificing
Their very life into his hands.

For one is quite dependent
On professional expertise
Whether suffering from pneumonia
Or a little cough or sneeze

Like lambs led to the slaughter
They fearfully await
A diagnosis from a doctor
And wonder have they come too late?

So make sure this doesn't happen
Keep your health on the right track
And ensure with every symptom shown
To your doctor you'll go back!

TRACTION ROOM
J.

Backache

I'm not trying to slack
I've this pain in my back
And I fear that my job is at risk
Things have got out of hand
It's quite awkward to stand
And I think I might have a slipped disc.

So I'm spending my days
Having tests and X-rays
No one seems the least sympathetic
You'd think I was faking
My poor back aching
And they expect me to be energetic!

Chiropractic and traction
Are part of the action
To set me in motion again
And to my surprise
I must exercise
In spite of my terrible pain.

Doctor says 'Not to worry
These things you can't hurry'
And he knows that they're on the right track
My recovery's assured
But if I'm not soon cured
I know I'll be facing the sack…

Well I'm feeling much better
For they've sent me a letter
And it's good news I think I deserve
My outlook is bright
For my back is alright
I've an inflamed sciatica nerve!

Cold or Flu?

I'm feeling ill and old
For I have this dreadful cold
In fact it's worse – I'm positive it's flu
I'm absolutely sure
That I have a temperature
And I feel that something serious is due.

My voice has turned quite hollow
And it's difficult to swallow
And that alone ensures it's tonsillitis
I've such pains in my head
That I've had to stay in bed
And I fear that by tonight I'll have bronchitis…

Will I get sympathy
If it turns to pleurisy?
My doctor, he'll just say that I'm neurotic
I know he wouldn't stay
If I had pneumonia on the way
He'll just prescribe a strong antibiotic!

Oh dear… I feel so blue
But doctor should be due
For I rang at half past nine and now it's five
I know I should endeavour
To pull myself together
I only hope he'll say that I'll survive!

He was in a tearing hurry
And he told me not to worry
He didn't even give me a prescription
'A little cold,' he said
'So keep warm and stay in bed'
No feeling for my horrible affliction…

Shall I take a vitamin
Or perhaps a double gin
Who knows, a little drink might drown my sorrow
Then I think perhaps I might
Regain my appetite
And feel a whole lot better by tomorrow!

Constipation

One day when I was feeling low
And finding it quite hard to 'go'
Though full of fear and trepidation
I bought this book on constipation.

It didn't take me long to find
That others have a sore 'behind'
So thought that I should take the time
To put my miseries down in rhyme.

It seems that if you have no urge
Then you should never, ever purge
But gently do it nature's way
To go quite comfortably each day.

Black molasses are the best
Taken at night before you rest
Even when you're on vacation
You're sure of an evacuation!

Figs, nuts and fruit containing seeds
Will minister to all your needs
And honey, bran and watercress
Will soon relieve your bowel distress.

So never take a pill or potion
To bring about that longed-for motion
Just heed the remedies I've told
And you'll go like a two-year-old!

Dulcie Levene

Frozen Shoulder

It's awful when you're older
To have a 'frozen shoulder'
Especially at night when you're in bed
In the morning when you're waking
You'll find that you are shaking
You can't lift your arm an inch above your head.

I seem unfortunate
For it's clearly been my fate
To be always having one thing or another
It was the same when I was small
From the moment I could crawl
I was a problem to my dear despairing mother.

Still it seems quite clear to me
I need physiotherapy
So I'm going to the hospital today
I've made up my mind to go
Although they're sick of me I know
But I'll stick it out whatever they might say.

They were kinder than I thought
So I think perhaps I ought
To stop moaning for a bit and do my best
They were really rather nice
So I'll follow their advice
And with their help let nature do the rest...

Dulcie Levene

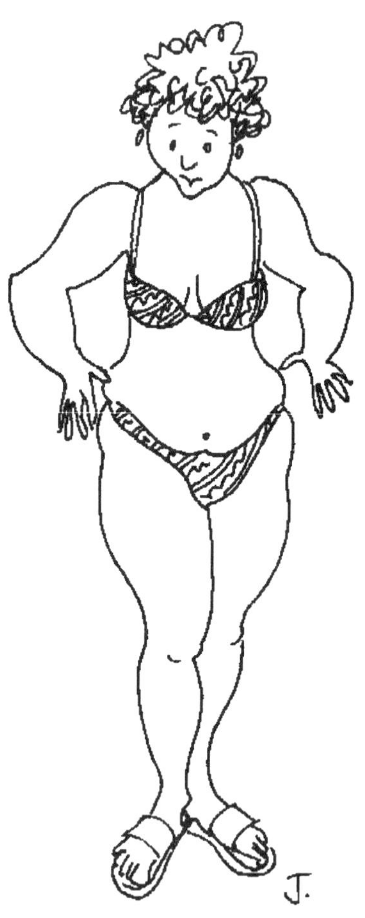

Slimming

I'm in a bad state
I'm two stone overweight
(It's the chocolate and cakes I consume)
But have I had a fright
For I looked such a sight
When I tried on my bathing costume!

No one could desire
Me! with my spare tyre
I'm the opposite of a trend setter
And my 'boobs' and my 'tum'
Not to mention my 'bum'
Well... the least said about them the better!

So I've started to slim
For I'd love to be trim
And it's health foods for me from today
No snacks watching 'telly'
Lemon tea and muesli...
And I'll get into shape... come what may!

Dulcie Levene

Piles

You can't be full of smiles
When you're suffering from 'piles'
Or, to be polite, a hemorrhoid condition
You can't sew or even knit
For it's difficult to sit
Quite hard to find a comfortable position…

You use suppositories and balm
To help you to stay calm
But the pain endured defies any description
So full of misery
You hurry to the surgery
And ask you doctor for a good prescription.

He probes internally
And says 'It's very plain to see
Your condition's painful but it isn't chronic
You have a strangulated pile
Which should disperse in just a while
And while you wait lay off that gin and tonic!'

EXIT
PATIENTS'
WAITING
ROOM

Friends

One's social life depends
On having lots of friends
And I haven't very many any more
Was it something that I said
They seem to absolutely dread
To see it's me when I knock on their door.

I'm good company I know
The conversation seems to flow
But after talking to me they all seem depressed
And I was told the other day
My dearest friend was heard to say
I'm a hypochondriac who's quite obsessed!

People always spoke to me
When I went to the surgery
They now get up and go the moment I am near
Patients that I sit beside
Seem to suddenly decide
They don't need to stay and quickly disappear!

A symptom shared or so they say
Can help a problem go away
So I'm just the one in whom they should confide
But some people are ungrateful
And one patient was quite hateful
And shouted at me, then broke down and cried!

I've had my cross to bear
And I only want to share
Any symptoms to alleviate their fear
They should think I'm very nice
To be offering advice
And be thankful for a sympathetic ear!

Dulcie Levene

Hope

It's a lovely day today
For Doctor's gone on holiday
And I've heard that there's a new one in his place
I think I'll go and see
If he'll examine me
So I'm going to take a bath now, just in case...

I hope he's nice to me
And shows some sympathy
I'll explain about my feelings of despair
Perhaps he'll understand
How my health's got out of hand
In fact I'm going to lay my soul quite bare...

He'll hear my tales of woe
And read my notes I know
And feel my worries and my dreadful state of mind
Perhaps I'll be assured
My condition can be cured
He'll be a lovely man, a doctor who is kind...

He was old and passed his prime
And said he didn't have the time
To treat imaginary illnesses like mine
'Count your blessings, dear,' he said
And think of someone else instead
And if you do you find you're feeling fine!

Dulcie Levene

Neighbours

I used to be friends
With the lady next door
Until she developed arthritis
Now I'm sorry to say
We don't speak any more
For I told her it could be phlebitis...

She called me a disgrace
Slammed the door in my face
And said I was a neighbour from Hell
Everyone in our street
Ignores me when we meet
And my husband's not talking as well...

So it's not very wise
To console or advise
As I've learned to my terrible cost
By trying to please
With my expertise
I can't count all the friendships I've lost!

So I've sent her a note
Saying I was unwise
My intentions were meant for the best
And I'd like to hear
If she had the 'All Clear'
When she got the results of her test…

She sent flowers today
With a message to say
Would we both go for supper tonight
Am I right to suspect
What I said was correct
And that my diagnosis was right?

Dulcie Levene

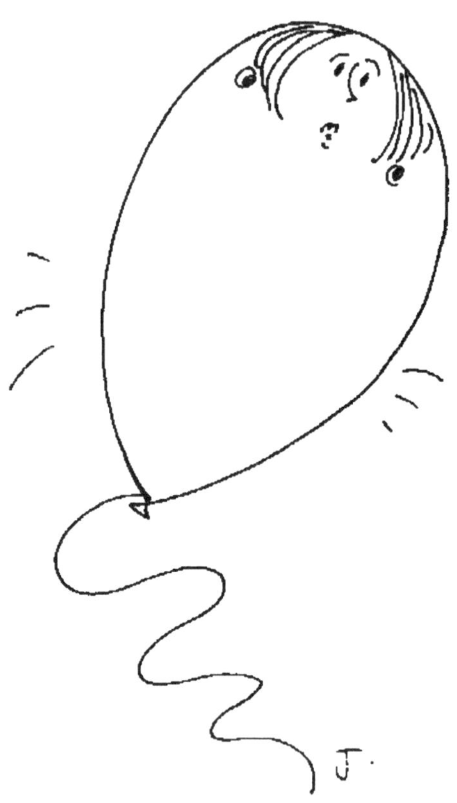

Wind

Don't feel that you have sinned
If you suddenly pass wind
After all it's quite a natural thing to do
For if you should restrain
You'll have the most appalling pain
And it's often difficult to find a 'loo'!

When reading you will see
That famous folk in history
Relieved themselves in front of congregations
And one very famous name
Who didn't feel a sense of shame
Listed Royals amongst his very close relations!

So next time you need to 'blow'
Well, take a chance and let it go
And if friends and family say, 'It isn't nice'
Volunteer this information
You've just had a consultation
And acting on your doctor's good advice!

Dulcie Levene

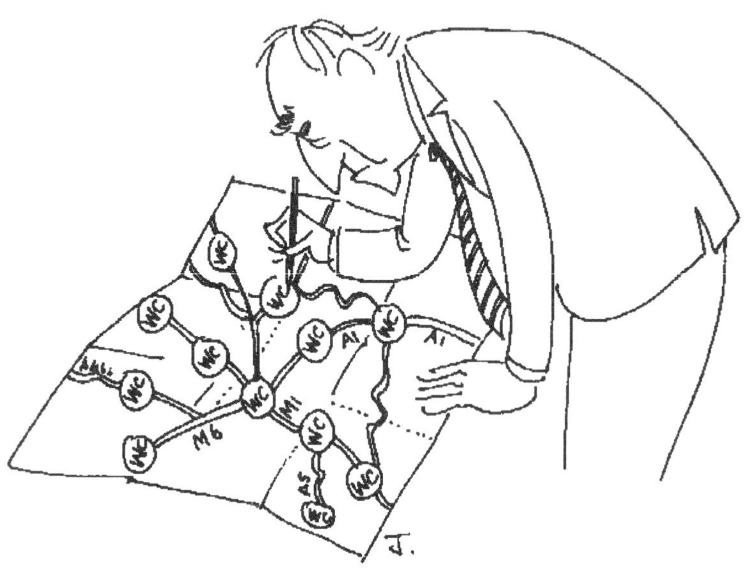

Prostate Gland

I'm feeling fine today
But my husband's not O.K.
His waterworks are getting out of hand
Our doctor's done his best
So now he's sent him for a test
For he fears that it could be his prostate gland…

When driving in the car
We don't travel very far
In case he has a horrible mishap
Conveniences for miles
Are listed in our notes and files
Gents' toilet zones pinpointed on our map

And he looks a dreadful sight
Well! he's up and down all night
I keep waking up and hoping it's a dream
Our lives are in a mess
And I know he's in distress
But if I hear that 'loo' flushed once again I'll scream!

He's filled with the neurotics
But he's on antibiotics
So perhaps they'll lift him out of his dejection
Oh! how I hope and pray
That they'll ring us up to say
It's just a nasty waterworks infection!

Dulcie Levene

Varicose Veins

I'm suffering with pains
For I have varicose veins
And my ankles look like puffy lumps of dough
I think perhaps I ought
To buy those stockings that support
Or black ones so the ugliness won't show…

I used to have such super 'pegs'
Why, years ago, for lovely legs
I won the 'Polly Perkins' lovelies competition
They'd have a shock I vow
If they could see my legs right now
They'd be appalled at their deplorable condition…

I'm living in anticipation
Of a marvelous operation
Which will help me have my 'Grable' legs again
A chance not to be missed
But… there's a three year waiting list
So I'll 'veinly' wait and try not to complain!

Waiting Room
SURGERY
J.

Conclusion

So now you've seen my little book
And read the tales I tell
I hope it brings you comfort
When you're not feeling very well.

And when you talk about your health
You must be most emphatic
That just because you worry
You're not hypochondriatic!

And if some people say you are
You shouldn't give a damn
Though now you've read my tales of woe
You probably think I am!

MEDICAL NOTES

Dear Doctor,

MEDICAL NOTES

Dear Doctor,